To, Da

Thank you for t.   ᵧₑₘₑ.

From, Del Boy x

Printed and published by J&B Print, Newton Stewart, 2021.

ISBN 978-1-8383847-3-9

CONTENTS

THANK YOU

Thank you for buying *First-Tee Winners (How to Win at Golf...Even When You Lose)* and for supporting the wonderful Junior Section at Swanston Golf Club.

Given that I'm trying to raise funds for junior golfers it would be a little odd to exclude them from the book by making the stories here too long or overly-complicated. For that reason, I have tried to write this book in a simple style that will appeal to confident young readers, possibly from around Primary 6 and up. However, I hope the stories in *First Tee Winners* are substantial enough for them to appeal to adults, as well.

Golf is a wonderful game. It can also be frustrating, irritating, infuriating, humbling and, if we are not careful, a little depressing! I hope you will find a story or two in *First-Tee Winners* that will re-ignite your golfing pilot light after a day or week or lifetime(!) of slicing, topping and three-putting.

Thank you to John at J and B Print for his patience and professionalism. Thank you to my front cover models, Shonagh, Aarron, and Jorja and to Jason Trench for his great cover photo....and they all waived their fees! I am grateful to Sam Sloan and Gerry Kelly of Blind Golf Scotland for their enthusiastic contributions. Thank you to Mike Robson, Manager at Swanston GC and my colleagues on our wee *"junior committee-type- thingy"* for their promises to help me flog some books!

A TEENY BIT WISER

I started playing golf when I was nine years old. I'm a bit embarrassed to admit that I've spent more than 40 years giving myself a very hard time for not winning trophies or medals or prizes. I've spoiled my own fun by trying much too hard and being super-critical of my own play.

I've spent most of my golfing life moaning, tutting and shaking my head. My expectations have been crazily high every time I've stepped on the first-tee. I've gone into deep huffs when I have failed to live up to them - which has been almost every time!

It was my Dad, Jim, who introduced me to golf. He was my biggest golfing rival and my best golfing pal. He was a mad-keen golfer and during his retirement he played four or five times each week, despite his failing health and knee-pain. Due to serious illness, my Dad's golfing journey came to a crashing stop. Sadly, he died last year. I've been thinking about him a lot. I've also been thinking that, perhaps, my golfing time is too precious to spend it moaning, tutting, shaking my head and feeling bad about myself!

I've spent over four decades thinking that golfing success is all about what we take from the course: things like trophies, medals, prizes and great scorecards. As I get older, and a teeny bit wiser, I'm starting to think that there may be more to winning at golf than that. Perhaps, being a winner is also about what we bring to the course, things like:

DETERMINATION   PATIENCE   HONESTY

FRIENDLINESS   RESILIANCE   KINDNESS

CALMNESS   SPORTING BEHAVIOUR

A SENSE OF FAIRNESS   A SENSE OF FUN

First-Tee Winners is a wee celebration of those qualities and more. Luckily, there are loads of great stories to tell!

IAN

Many years ago, I was a member of a golf club in a small town in Galloway in south-west Scotland. There was a young man who played there, called Ian, who had a physical disability and speech difficulties. Ian's physical disability meant he had to play golf with only his right hand. That's not easy!

Ian also had mobility problems and he found playing eighteen holes on this hilly course very tiring; he would really struggle for energy towards the end of a round and it was often obvious that he was experiencing pain in his legs. He battled through and rarely, if ever, quit before completing all eighteen holes.

Ian refused to let the obstacles he faced hold him back. Ian wanted to take part, to be involved. He got an official golf handicap (the maximum was 28 back then) and played in competitions from the same medal tees as everyone else.

Ian wanted to win, too! However, from what I can remember, Ian never won a trophy or a medal during the years I played there. He never stopped trying.

It would be ridiculous, and a little cruel, to think of Ian as a golfing *"loser"* simply because he never won a trophy. Through golf, Ian demonstrated determination, endurance and a stubborn refusal to be limited by his physical difficulties. I believe Ian <u>was</u> a *"winner"* every time he stood on the first-tee with his can-do spirit, ready to take on the challenge of golf.

Although he doesn't know it yet, Ian inspired my *First-Tee Winners* idea. A First-Tee Winner is a golfer who brings admirable and impressive personal qualities to the first-tee.

Whatever their golfing ability may be, a First-Tee Winner arrives at the course with an exceptional character, attitude or personality. Ian's name may not be engraved on any trophies or inscribed on a champions board but Ian was a special kind of winner - a First-Tee Winner.

BEING A WINNER ISN'T ALL ABOUT LEAVING WITH THE TROPHY. BEING A WINNER IS ALSO ABOUT WHAT WE BRING TO THE FIRST-TEE...OUR CHARACTER, ATTITUDE AND PERSONALITY.

FIRST-TEE WINNERS, LIKE IAN, FACE UP TO DIFFICULT CHALLENGES. THEIR LOVE OF GOLF IS BIGGER AND STRONGER THAN ANY OF THE OBSTACLES THAT STAND IN THEIR WAY.

23 OUT OF 100 IS AWESOME!

If you scored 23 out of 100 in a school maths test your Mum and Dad might (calmly!) suggest that you need to do some serious swotting. If you are an adult, and enjoy a pub quiz, you know that 23 out of 100 isn't going to win the beers.

In any test or competition or situation 23 out of 100 is not great - in fact, it's really pretty poor. EXCEPT IN GOLF! In golf, 23 out of 100 is AWESOME!

23 out of 100 (23%) is the highest win rate of any professional golfer...EVER! Annika Sorenstam played in 307 professional events and won 72 of them, giving her that top-of-the class win rate of 23%. Here are the win rates of the two best male golfers ever, Tiger Woods and Jack Nicklaus...

Tiger Woods (22%) – he loses 78 out of 100 competitions that he plays.

Jack Nicklaus (12%) – he lost 88 out of 100 competitions that he played.

Rory McIlroy, Britain's best golfer of recent years, loses around 90 times in 100.

Nelly Korda, who topped the women's world rankings in 2021, loses around 93 times in 100, as does Dustin Johnson, who has spent over 130 weeks as the No1 male golfer.

Why does any of this matter? Because golf is a humbling game for everyone and if we judge our success solely on our tournament victories, we are going to spend an awful lot of our golfing time feeling disappointed, frustrated or even angry... I should know!

The difficulty with winning golf competitions is that everyone else who is playing is trying to stop you! The good news is that no-one can stop you from adopting a winning attitude and becoming a First-Tee Winner.

NO MATTER HOW GOOD, OR GREAT, WE GET AT GOLF WE WILL LOSE MANY MORE COMPETITIONS THAN WE WIN.

LOTS OF PLAYERS CAN STOP YOU FROM WINNING TROPHIES. NO-ONE CAN STOP YOU FROM HAVING FUN AND TRYING YOUR BEST.

YOU <u>CAN'T</u> CHOOSE TO WIN. YOU <u>CAN</u> CHOOSE TO BECOME A FIRST-TEE WINNER WITH A GREAT ATTITUDE.

YOUR NEXT BIG "*WIN*"

I said earlier that Ian from my hometown never won a trophy. However, I can clearly remember the evening when Ian and his partner scored well and were one of six pairs in the club to qualify for the County Two-Ball Final. Ian's smile that evening was as big as any I've ever seen from Tiger Woods. Qualifying for the County Two-Ball Final <u>was</u> Ian's big win.

That's one of the wonderful things about golf – with effort we can win our own battles with the game and with ourselves, even when we don't win the trophy...

"I've broken 90!".

"My drive at the 6th got over that sneaky little stream!".

"My handicap has dropped by a whole stroke this month!".

"I've finally beaten Laura!".

"I shot 10 at the 2nd and I didn't give in, like I would have in the past!".

"I've been very ill lately but today I managed to play nine holes!".

"I've qualified for the club championship!"

"I chipped in today...I've never done that before!"

"I've been practising my putting a lot...and I didn't three-putt today!".

"We've qualified for the County Two-Ball Final!"

FIRST-TEE WINNERS UNDERSTAND THAT THEY CAN'T ALWAYS WIN TROPHIES AND MEDALS, SO THEY TAKE PRIDE IN, AND GREAT SATISFACTION FROM, THEIR PERSONAL *"WINS"*.

KEEP A LOOK-OUT FOR <u>YOUR</u> NEXT BIG *"WIN"*...AND ENJOY IT!

THE *"BIGGER PICTURE"*

Before telling you about some very famous First Tee Winners, I want to tell you who Ian's partner was the night that he qualified for the County Two-Ball Final. It was my Dad, Jim.

My Dad loved golf and was fiercely competitive. I've never seen anyone try so hard to win £1 in a Friday evening *"bounce"* game! He got down to a five or six handicap, won a few trophies, played numerous times for the club team and had 13 holes-in-one. I haven't had any...yet!

My Dad partnered Ian in a lot of pairs events. I don't mean to be nasty to Ian but this did reduce my Dad's chances of winning, because Ian would often get very nervous or tired or both and if his ball went into thick rough, or a bunker, it was almost impossible for him to get it out. My Dad didn't mind one little bit.

I think my Dad was a First-Tee Winner because to him making Ian feel wanted and included was more important than winning. He could see the *"bigger picture"*. That's a great attitude to bring to the first-tee.

WINNING COMPETITIONS IS IMPORTANT TO A FIRST-TEE WINNER BUT IT IS NO MORE IMPORTANT THAN MAKING FRIENDS AND HELPING OTHERS.

THE 10,000% GOLFER

Tiger Woods is the most famous golfing superstar of all time. The printer who printed this book would have to order a lot more paper for me to list all of Tiger's incredible achievements. I'll save a few trees and just say that Tiger has won 15 major titles, a record-equalling 82 events on the US PGA Tour and squillions of dollars in prizemoney.

The thing that I really want to tell you about is the day that Tiger scored ten on a par 3. Yes, you read it correctly...

TIGER SCORED TEN - YES, 10! ON A PAR 3!!!

This happened at the 12th hole of the Augusta National course during the final round of the 2020 US Masters. Tiger wasn't amongst the leaders when he stepped on to the 12th tee but after hitting three balls into the pond in front of the green any hope that he had of a Top 10, or Top 20, finish was gone. It was shocking that the great Tiger Woods would shoot seven over par on one hole. But here's how Tiger responded...

13th – birdie   14th – par   15th – birdie

16th – birdie   17th – birdie   18th – birdie

Tiger doesn't know what *"give up"* means. Or *"give in"*. Or *"stop trying"*. Or *"surrender"*. Or *"switch off"*. Or *"sulk"*.

Tiger has a wonderful win rate of (over) 22%, the second-best in history. Tiger has an effort rate of **10,000%**:

100% effort x 100% of the time = 10,000%

Tiger has said:

"My parents told me that it was OK to fail, as long as I gave it everything I had. I have given it everything I had".

> **FIRST-TEE WINNERS ARE PROUD GOLFERS. THEY ARE PROUD OF THEIR TALENT, THEIR SKILL AND THEIR WINS. MOST OF ALL, THEY ARE PROUD OF THE EFFORT THEY MAKE ON EVERY SHOT, UNTIL THE FINAL PUTT DROPS.**

Tiger wasn't born a 10,000% golfer. Tiger learned to be that way at an early age. When he was eleven years old, Tiger played in the Optimist Junior World Championship in San Diego. Tiger came up against a player who was taller and stronger than him. When his opponent drove the green at the short par 4 first hole, Tiger was astounded – he had never seen such power in a junior player. When the boy holed out for a birdie to win the hole, Tiger convinced himself he couldn't win and he gave up.

Tiger lost that match but the defeat taught him to try his best on every shot, no matter what. It certainly worked over the thirty years that followed!

THE GIRL WHO MISSED HER PUTTS...ON PURPOSE!

Annika Sorenstam was born in Sweden in 1970. Annika was a very shy girl. She was bright at school but didn't like to put her hand up in class to answer questions; she was frightened that her classmates would laugh at her if she gave the wrong answer.

At around the age of 12-years-old Annika's parents introduced her to golf. Annika loved it, improved quickly and soon realised that she was good enough to win junior events.

There was one big problem! The winners of junior competitions had to make a short speech after being presented with their prize. Annika really didn't want to do that! In fact, the thought of making a speech in front of other players and their parents frightened her very much.

Annika came up with a cunning plan. She would play as well as she could for 14 or 15 holes but in the last few holes Annika would start to miss putts...on purpose! By doing that she had a good chance of winning the second or third prize but she wouldn't need to make a speech.

Eventually Annika's parents and the Junior Organisers noticed this pattern in her play and became suspicious. They came up with their own cunning plan! At the next tournament Annika finished second and was told that she <u>had</u> to make a speech. There was no escape. Anika was *"terrified"* and her heart was jumping out of her chest *"like a cartoon character"* but she said a few words. She wasn't harmed or hurt or laughed at. She didn't enjoy the experience but she felt ok.

Annika realised that public speaking wasn't really as terrifying as she had feared. She stopped missing putts on purpose. She started enjoying golf more than ever. She started winning...and didn't stop! In fact, Annika went on to become one of the best golfers in the history of the game.

Despite having to make dozens of winner's speeches in her career, Annika never became a very confident public speaker. However, she learned to accept that speaking in public is part of being a champion golfer. Years later this is what Annika said about her first ever speech:

"That's when I realised, I had to face my fears. If you want to achieve something in life you have to just overcome some of the things that you feel uncomfortable with...".

FIRST-TEE WINNERS EXPERIENCE FEAR, WORRY AND STRESS. THEY LEARN TO FACE UP TO THESE FEELINGS AND COPE WITH THEM AS BEST THEY CAN...JUST LIKE THAT SHY, WEE, SWEDISH GIRL DID.

THE JUG AND THE JACKET

When Adam Scott arrived on the 15th tee of the final round of the 2012 Open Championship with a four shot lead it seemed certain that he would win his first major title and get his hands on the Claret Jug, the oldest trophy in professional golf. At the time Adam was ranked the 13th best player in the world and had already won over twenty professional tournaments. He was hugely talented with the smoothest swing on the planet.

What could possibly go wrong? Lots! Adam scored bogey (one over par) on every one of the last four holes and lost by one stroke to Ernie Els. Adam's last four holes have been described as one of the worst *"collapses"* in Open championship history.

Adam then had to answer questions from golf journalists and TV channels. He looked shocked and extremely disappointed (understatement of the year!), but this is what he said...

"I know I've let a really great chance slip through my fingers today but, you know, somehow I'll look back and take the positives from it. I don't think I've ever played this well in a major championship, so that's a good thing for me moving forward. All the stuff I'm doing is going in the right direction".

Despite the pain of the most bitter disappointment of his career, Adam could still see that he was getting better. Adam praised himself and built up his self-esteem when he needed it most. Adam knew what he had to say about himself, and to himself, to ensure that he turned a terrible disappointment into something that would eventually help him progress.

In April 2013, only nine months after his so-called *"collapse"* at The Open, Adam became the first Australian to win the US Masters. He was now a major winner and the proud owner of the famous green jacket.

Adam did *"lose"* The Open - he certainly let it slip through his fingers - but he never thought of himself as a *"loser."*

"LOSING" **IS A SINGLE EVENT THAT HAPPENS TO YOU ON A PARTICULAR DAY. BEING A** *"LOSER"* **IS A NEGATIVE, PESSIMISTIC, BITTER, UNGRATEFUL OR ANGRY ATTITUDE THAT YOU CARRY AROUND EVERY DAY.**

FIRST-TEE WINNERS LOSE A LOT OF COMPETITIONS (THAT'S HOW GOLF IS!) BUT ALWAYS TRY HARD TO AVOID THINKING OR BEHAVING LIKE A *"LOSER".*

FROM MASTERS CRASH TO MASTERCLASS

No-one could identify more with Adam Scott's four-bogies-in-a-row collapse at the 2012 Open Championship than his fellow top pro, Northern Irishman, Rory McIlroy, who endured a similar fate a little over a year earlier.

After three rounds of the 2011 US Masters, Rory had a four-shot lead at twelve under par. He seemed destined to win his first major championship and to slip on the famous US Masters green jacket, at the age of 21.

After nine holes of his final round Rory's lead had been cut to one shot. Then came one of the most jaw-dropping meltdowns in major championship history. Rory hit a vicious hook off the 10th tee and took a triple bogey seven. He bogeyed the 11th. At the par 3 12th, he took four putts from around 25 feet for a double-bogey 5. When he hooked his tee-shot at the 13th into Rae's Creek, Rory looked close to tears.

Rory finished ten shots behind the winner, Charl Schwartzel. His 80 was the worst final round by a third-round leader in US Masters history.

Many commentators and journalists said that young Rory would never psychologically recover from such a monumental collapse. Doom-mongers predicted that his career would come to an immediate crashing halt. However, only a few days after his Masters meltdown Rory gave this masterclass in sporting behaviour, maturity, patience, optimism and confidence, when speaking to *Telegraph.co.uk:*

"I've known Charl for a long time and I'm happy for him…. He played great on Sunday, to go out and shoot 66 in the final day of the Masters and win was a great performance. I'll have plenty of chances to get my hands on that green jacket…Obviously I was very disappointed at the time but these things happen and it's not the end of the world… I've just got to stay patient…"

So much for Rory being psychologically damaged!

That interview with *The Telegraph* wasn't Rory's final masterclass of 2011. Exactly ten weeks after crumbling at the US Masters, Rory won the US Open – one of the four major championships in the men's game. Not only did Rory win, he did so with a US Open record score of 268, giving him an eight-shot winning margin. At 22 years-old, Rory became the youngest winner of the US Open since Bobby Jones in 1923.

So much for Rory's career coming to a crashing halt!

> **FIRST-TEE WINNERS DON'T PAY ATTENTION TO THE NEGATIVITY AND PESSIMISM OF OTHERS. THEY BELIEVE IN THEMSELVES.**

NO HAMMER REQUIRED

Justin Rose finished joint fourth in the 1998 Open Championship when he was a 17-year-old amateur player. It was the best finish in The Open by an amateur in 45 years. Had Britain discovered its own Tiger Woods?

Justin gave up his amateur status immediately and four days after The Open he competed in the Dutch Open as a professional. Events on the European Tour are played over 72 holes – 18 holes per day from Thursday to Sunday. After the first two rounds a *"cut"* is made. This means that the 65 players with the best scores qualify to play on Saturday and Sunday. Players who don't qualify are said to *"miss the cut"*; they are out of the tournament and win no money.

Justin missed the cut at the Dutch Open. In his second event, he missed the cut. In his third event it happened again. Then it happened again. And again. And again. And again.

Justin Rose, the young Englishman who looked like he may be golf's next superstar at The Open, missed 21 cuts in a row...yes, 21! 21 professional events, 21 missed cuts - and not one penny in prize-money!

Here is how Justin coped during this incredibly challenging and frustrating time in his early professional career:

"I started to not judge myself on making the cut. I started to judge myself on 'Am I making improvements?' So, if I missed the cut by seven one week and I go out the next week and play

a bit better I'd say 'Ok, you're getting there, you missed the cut by four, things are moving' I wouldn't hammer myself further into the ground...I started to build it the other way".

Justin never reached for a mental hammer to bash himself down with. He tried to build himself up with positive self-talk, optimism and self-respect.

It worked...eventually! Justin won his first professional event in 2002. Since then, Justin has won many events including the 2013 US Open and a gold medal at the 2016 Rio Summer Olympics. In 2018 he reached No1 in the world rankings.

Justin has a win-rate of around 4%. Judging by his TV interviews he has a patience and politeness rate of 100%.

> **FIRST-TEE WINNERS DON'T BRING A MENTAL HAMMER TO THE FIRST-TEE. THEY UNDERSTAND THAT GOLF IS TOUGH AND BEATING THEMSELVES UP AFTER POOR SHOTS, OR ROUNDS, ISN'T GOING TO MAKE IT EASIER!**

BEATING THE BULLIES

Haley Moore was born in the state of Illinois, USA in 1998. Haley has always been large for her age. Throughout her school years she was often called *"fat"* and *"ugly"* by classmates. When she sat down to eat in the school canteen, pupils sitting at that table would often move to another one. For a long time, Haley didn't tell her parents what was going on.

On one occasion a group of boys snatched Haley's school backpack and filled it with water, ruining her favourite book. Naturally, Haley broke down. Haley told her Mum, who met with the school headteacher and things improved a little. However, Haley spent most of her school years being laughed at, taunted, insulted and rejected.

Through a visit to a driving range with her family, Haley discovered golf. Haley instantly fell in love with the *"quiet and control"* of the game and played often. She felt powerful as she thrashed balls on the range. Haley also enjoyed the compliments she received from other golfers, such as: *"Wow, great swing!"*.

Sadly, golf wasn't a complete escape from the bullies. Hayley improved very quickly and was much more powerful than other players of her age. Many junior golfers were envious of her power and skill and were mean to her.

None of this stopped Haley from becoming one of the best junior players in the USA. As a 16-year-old, Haley qualified for the 2015 ANA Inspiration, which is one of the five major events in the women's professional game. Haley was the only amateur to *"make the cut"* (i.e. qualify for the final two rounds).

However, having suffered years of bullying, Haley became her own worst bully. She expected great things from herself and was rarely pleased with her on-course efforts. She became a self-critical and angry golfer.

As a shy 17-year-old, Haley began attending the University of Arizona. Laura Ianello, the University's head golf coach, has said that many of the girls in the golf team didn't accept Haley; it took eighteen months for her to settle into the golf team and to be accepted.

During her time at the University of Arizona, Haley's big moment of golfing glory came in the final of the of 2018 National Collegiate Athletic Association (NCAA) Championship against the University of Alabama. At the first hole of sudden-death, Haley holed a five-foot putt to win the championship for the Arizona "Wildcats".

If you want to witness 15 seconds of pure golfing joy, check out the YouTube video of Haley holing her winning putt. You will smile, I promise!

Haley graduated in 2019. She turned professional and won two events on the Cactus Tour. In November 2020, Haley achieved her dream of qualifying for the Ladies Professional Golf Association (LPGA) Tour (at her first attempt!).

A few weeks later, Haley was interviewed by Robin Roberts on *Good Morning, America* and said this....

"I had a really good slogan growing up, which was 'DREAM. BELIEVE. ACHIEVE'. So, I had a dream of making it to the LPGA tour and to do that I had to believe in myself and if I had obstacles come in front of me, which I did, I Knew I just had to keep fighting and be strong…"

Haley had this advice for kids who are struggling with bullying:

"…don't let other people judge you by how you look, if you talk different or if you look different than any other boys or girls. You be you".

> **FIRST-TEE WINNERS AREN'T UNFEELING ROBOTS. THEY ARE NORMAL HUMAN-BEINGS, WITH NORMAL EMOTIONS. THEY GET HURT BY ABUSE, BULLYING OR REJECTION. THEY GET DOWN…BUT THEY DON'T <u>STAY</u> DOWN.**

HEADS HELD HIGH

When he reached the ninth tee of the final round of the 2006 Irish Open, Darren Clarke had a two-shot lead. The conditions were horrible – pouring rain, fierce winds and darkening skies. Darren sliced his drive into very long, thick rough which the Sky TV commentator described as *"horrid"*. When he got to his ball, it was obvious to Darren that all he could do was wedge it out on to the fairway. However, the hooter blew to suspend play for the day and Darren didn't get a chance to play his shot.

When Darren returned to his ball the next morning, he discovered something peculiar: the grass around his ball had been flattened and his lie was now much better than it had been the day before. Although no-one is certain, it is likely that some Irish fans thought they would give the likeable Northern Irishman a helping-hand by flattening the grass.

Darren is a very powerful player and with his improved lie he felt able to muscle a mid-iron on to the front of the green. He was free to do so – he hadn't broken any rules, because it wasn't him who improved his lie.

Darren didn't muscle an iron on to the green. He took out a wedge and knocked the ball 50 yards up the fairway – exactly the shot that he would have played the day before. He didn't have to, but he did. Darren chose not to benefit from the help the local fans had given him. This is what Darren later wrote about this incident:

"Instead of going for the green, I hit the shot that I would have hit the night before. If I had

gone for the green and then proceeded to win the tournament, I would never have forgiven myself... my conscience was clear...You either win fairly and squarely or not at all. Your results should be a true reflection of how you've played, not how you've abused or broken the rules".

Darren finished third that week. He didn't walk away with the trophy but he did walk away with his head held high.

English golfer, Brian Davis also did something wonderfully honest in a sudden-death play-off at the 2010 Verizon Heritage Tournament. Although no-one else saw him do it, Brian accidently touched a loose reed of grass with his club whilst playing a shot from a water hazard. This was against the rules. Brian immediately called a two-shot penalty on himself. He lost the hole and tournament to Jim Furyk. This is how Brian explained his decision to penalise himself:

"Well, obviously I want to win a PGA Tour event more than just about anything but no victory would be worthwhile if it had a cloud hanging over it...I am proud to uphold the values that my parents taught me and I teach my kids the same stuff. Be honest in your sport and simply try your best".

Brian has played in hundreds of events and has won two. His win rate is not particularly impressive. His honesty is.

WINNING TROPHIES IS IMPORTANT TO A FIRST-TEE WINNER BUT IT IS NOT NEARLY AS IMPORTANT AS PLAYING FAIRLY AND ACTING HONESTLY.

ANY PLAYER WHO BRINGS A STRONG SENSE OF HONESTY, DECENCY AND FAIRNESS TO THE FIRST-TEE CAN NEVER BE DESCRIBED AS A *"LOSER"*.

FIRST-TEE WINNERS CARE MUCH MORE ABOUT THEIR CHARACTER THAN THEIR WIN-RATE.

"NICE GUYS FINISH LAST...BLAH, BLAH, BLAH"

You may have heard the saying, _"nice guys finish last"_. It means that a polite, kind, thoughtful, fair and gentle person cannot possibly succeed in sport or work or life. It promotes the idea that to succeed, you need to be nasty, hard, aggressive, ruthless and unfeeling. It is utter nonsense.

Jack Nicklaus won 18 major golf events in his career. That's three more than his nearest rival, Tiger Woods. Amazingly, Jack finished second in 19 majors. Between 1960 and 1982, Jack played in 88 majors and had 66 Top 10 finishes. Awesome.

Many golf lovers believe that Jack is the greatest male golfer of all time. Also, he earned huge respect, and made many friends, because of his thoughtfulness, fairness and sporting behaviour. Here is a flavour of what fellow golfers have said about Jack...

**GREG NORMAN: "Jack sat down with me in the locker room at my first Australian Open and encouraged me. When I was anxious at my first Masters, he put his arm around me and mentioned that he was nervous too. When I was leading the 1986 British Open going into the final day, he pulled up a chair at dinner the night before and offered me some advice. The next day, when I won, he went out of his way to congratulate me".**

LAURA DAVIES: *"Jack Nicklaus is a wonderful man".*

LEE TREVINO: *"Jack Nicklaus had a lot of influence on me. We were playing a charity match...and he sat me down in the locker room for a talk. I've always worshipped that man... 'You don't know how good a player you are' he told me, 'You can win anywhere'. I thought about that and it turned me around".*

TOM WATSON: *"You take a lot of different paths in life. There's no doubt one of the best ones I took was becoming Jack's friend".*

GARY PLAYER: *"Jack never made any bones about the fact that he wanted to beat your brains out on the golf course, but when he came out on the short end of the fight, he unfailingly conducted himself with grace and honor...In this regard, Jack has been a model for his contemporaries, such as myself, and the players who have come after him".*

The idea that *"nice guys finish last"* can be disproved with two words: Jack Nicklaus.

FIRST-TEE WINNERS ARE <u>ALWAYS</u> MENTALLY TOUGH: DETERMINED, PERSISTANT, PATIENT, RESILIANT AND FOCUSED. THEY ARE <u>NEVER</u> DESPERATE, SELF-OBSESSED, DISHONEST, NASTY OR CRUEL.

STANDING ON THE FIRST-TEE, A FIRST-TEE WINNER KNOWS EXACTLY HOW THE GAME WILL END...WITH A HANDSHAKE, *"WELL PLAYED"* AND *"THANKS FOR THE GAME"*.

"THE CONCESSION"

In the previous section, we saw that Jack Nicklaus, arguably the greatest male golfer of all time, earned a reputation for being calm, polite and generous in defeat, sporting in victory and always supportive of his fellow players.

The finest example of Jack's gentlemanly behaviour came at the 1969 Ryder Cup at Royal Birkdale, England. Britain hadn't beaten the USA in the Ryder Cup since 1957 and had been soundly beaten in the five matches prior to 1969. When Jack and his opponent, Tony Jacklin, reached the 18th hole of the final match of the 1969 contest both their match and the overall match score were all square. The 10,000-strong British crowd were desperate for a long-overdue Ryder Cup victory, if only Tony could win the final hole.

Jack put an end to those hopes when he rolled in a five-foot putt on the 18th for a four. Tony was left with a two-foot putt for his four, to halve his match with Jack and to halve the overall contest 16-16. If Tony had missed the putt, Britain would have lost the Ryder Cup for the seventh consecutive time and he would have felt terrible.

That didn't happen. Jack bent over, picked up Tony's ball-marker and shook his hand saying:

"I don't think you would have missed that Tony, but I didn't want to give you the chance".

Jack had conceded Tony's short putt (as is allowed in match play). Tony and Jack's match was halved. The Ryder Cup finished 16-16. America, as defending champions, retained the trophy.

The American captain, Sam Snead, and many of the American players, were furious at Jack for conceding a putt that could have been missed in such a high-pressure situation. The USA side had come to England to win the Ryder Cup outright, *"not be good ol' boys"*, according to Sam Snead.

Over fifty years later, Jack's act of sportsmanship at the 1969 Ryder Cup remains part of golfing folklore. It is still held up as one of the finest acts of sporting behaviour in the long history of the game. In an instant, Jack had calculated that a tied match was the best and fairest result for him and Tony, the Ryder Cup and the wider game of golf.

The thing that impresses me most about Jack's act is that Tony Jacklin had already beaten Jack earlier that day in the morning singles. It wasn't a narrow victory for the Englishman – he won in fine fashion, four up with three holes to play. Of course, Jack wanted to *"get his own back"* in their afternoon match but he wasn't desperate to do so...as his generous concession at the eighteenth hole demonstrated.

Jack's self-esteem and self-image as a person didn't revolve around winning a golf match. He *wanted* to win. He didn't *need* to win to feel good about himself. If he did, *"The Concession"* would never have happened.

TIGER'S *"GRANDPA CHARLIE"*

Charlie Sifford was born in 1922 and raised in Charlotte, North Carolina. Charlie's family lived close to the Carolina Country Club and, aged ten, Charlie started caddying there along with other black boys and men. Charlie was proud that he was able to earn money and contribute to his family's income.

The Carolina Country Club allowed caddies to play the course on Mondays. Charlie loved to play. By the age of around fifteen he was regularly playing the course in par, despite using borrowed clubs. When he was around 16 years-old Charlie was suddenly told by the club that he could no longer play on the course. No explanation was given. Charlie had done nothing wrong.

In 1939 Charlie moved north to Philadelphia to live with his uncle and got a job in a factory, where he worked for over three years. One morning he saw a man jumping aboard a streetcar with golf clubs on his shoulder. Charlie followed him to Cobbs Creek public golf course, where black and white players played alongside each other. Charlie rediscovered his love of golf and Cobbs Creek became his second home. Charlie honed his skills there, playing, and beating, some of the finest black golfers in the state.

After serving his country during World War II, Charlie turned professional in 1948. He played on the United Golfers Association (UGA) Tour, a professional tour set up by and for black golfers, with tournaments held on public courses. Charlie won the UGA National Negro Open from 1952 to 1956 then reclaimed it in 1960.

Charlie loved to compete and he loved to win but he wanted to test himself against America's best golfers, black and white. However, Charlie's ambition to compete against white players was largely thwarted by Article III, Section I of the constitution of the Professional Golfers Association (PGA) of America. This stated that only *"Caucasian"* (white) players were eligible for membership. Charlie, and other top black golfers, couldn't compete on the PGA Tour because of the colour of their skin. It was there in the rules, ironically, in black and white.

After a campaign led by boxing legend (and golf obsessive) Joe Louis, seven black golfers (including Charlie) got a chance to qualify for the 1952 Phoenix Open. Charlie and the other black players were put together in the first two groups. When Charlie got to the first green, he found that the hole was full of human excrement. He was so shocked and angered by this that he couldn't concentrate properly and he failed to qualify.

Charlie occasionally got the opportunity to play in some important tournaments with mixed fields. He shot 63 in the first round of the 1955 Canadian Open and led the field, which included a young Arnold Palmer (who went on to become a golfing legend). In 1957, Charlie won the Long Beach Open, becoming the first African-American to win an open tournament against a field that included many of the country's best golfers. The event was co-sponsored by the PGA but was not an official PGA event because it was only 54 holes long. Charlie finished 32nd in the 1959 US Open.

Charlie remained incredibly frustrated that he was reliant on the invitation of a handful of liberal-minded, forward-thinking tournament organisers and event sponsors. The hard fact remained that Charlie had no *"right"* to play in PGA events, purely because of his race.

Stanley Mosk, the white attorney general of California took up Charlie's case and waged a battled against the PGA over their racially discriminatory practices. He threatened to ban the PGA from holding events in California. Initially, Charlie was made an *"approved"* PGA member, with limited playing rights. On the 9th November 1961, following increased pressure from Stanley Mosk, the *"Caucasian-only"* clause was officially removed from the PGA's rulebook. Charlie became a member of the PGA Tour, the first person of colour to do so.

Even after becoming an official PGA Tour pro, Charlie continued to face discrimination, mistreatment and abuse. At tournaments, he was often refused service at the host club's bar and dining room and was forced to eat his meals in the locker room. He was regularly taunted or abused on the course, whilst trying to concentrate and make a living for his wife and family.

In 1961 Charlie made his homecoming as a PGA pro when he played in the Greater Greensboro Open in North Carolina. It was an invitational event and he received an invitation only because of the effort of a friend and activist called Dr George Simkins. North Carolina is one of the USA's southern states where, at that time, racism was even more entrenched than it was in the north. Very few hotels in the city would accept African-Americans guests. A friend of Dr Simkins provided Charlie with a room. Charlie shot 68 (three under) in the opening round. That evening he received a threatening telephone call telling him to stay away from the tournament: *"don't come tomorrow if you know what's good for you"*.

Charlie was frightened but he wanted to play and needed to play to make a living. Despite his fears, Charlie played. He was followed around the course by a group of around one dozen white men who taunted him, called him disgusting names and did everything they could to put him off. Charlie recognised the voice of one of the men; he was the man who had threatened him on the telephone the previous evening. After fourteen holes the men were eventually escorted from the course by the police. Charlie couldn't understand why it had taken the police so long to act.

Charlie drew on the advice he had received in 1948 from Jackie Robinson, the USA's first black professional baseball player, to remain cool and calm even when he felt like fighting back. Although he was incredibly angry, Charlie knew that if he retaliated, even only verbally, he, and every other black player, would have been punished by getting even less access to the big events.

Amazingly, Charlie finished the 1961 Greensboro Open tied fourth. He has said:

"I hadn't won the tournament in Greensboro, but I felt a larger victory. I had come through my first southern tournament with the worst kind of social pressures and discrimination around me, and I hadn't cracked. I hadn't quit".

Charlie continued to play. In August 1967, just after his 45th birthday, Charlie won his first full PGA event shooting 64 in final round of Greater Hartford Open. When he was handed his $20,000 winner's cheque, Charlie could barely fight back the tears and said:

"If you try hard enough, anything can happen".

Charlie went on to win the Los Angeles Open two years later, aged 47. He would amass more than $340,000 on the PGA Tour and $1million on the Senior PGA Tour. The sad truth, however, is that Charlie's finest golfing days were almost over by the time he had been granted PGA membership. Charlie had spent his best, fittest, strongest years as a golfer travelling all around the country trying to find tournaments that he could compete in. It is perhaps no surprise that Charlie called his 1992 autobiography *Just Let Me Play*.

In 2004 Charlie became the first black inductee of the World Golf Hall of Fame. In 2014 President Obama presented Charlie with a Presidential Medal of Freedom. He accepted these honours with gratitude and dignity.

Shortly after he turned professional, Tiger Woods met with Charlie. The two men became very close friends. Charlie saw Tiger as an adopted grandson and Tiger began to call him *"Grandpa Charlie"*. When Tiger and his (then) wife Elin had a son in 2009, he was named Charlie after Charlie Sifford.

Although he had an especially close bond with Charlie, Tiger is aware that there have been many black golfers, men and women, whose talent was not given free reign due to racial injustice. Tiger has written:

"Golf has afforded me a stage for free expression. That freedom, however, was a gift paid for by many determined people who endured all kinds of indignities just to be able to play the game. I and every person of colour who enjoys this great game can do so because of their determination and grit. I'm reminded of that every time I tee it up".

SOME GOLFERS HAVE ENDURED YEARS OF GREAT CHALLENGE, OUTRAGEOUS ABUSE AND GROSS INJUSTICE SIMPLY TO MAKE IT TO THE FIRST-TEE. NO MATTER WHAT THEIR TROPHY COUNT, OR WIN-RATE, MAY BE, THESE GOLFERS ARE AMONGST THE GREATEST *"WINNERS"* IN THE HISTORY OF THE GAME.

PAINFUL JOURNEYS

Stacey Lewis is an American professional golfer who has won thirteen tour events, including two majors. In 2013 she became the No1 ranked woman golfer in the world. That's pretty impressive. Add in the fact that, at eleven years-old, she was diagnosed with scoliosis (a sideways curving of the spine) and Stacey's story becomes amazing.

The LPGA's website has lots of inspiring stories from great players, under the title *Drive On* – a celebration of *"hard work, focus and tenacity"*. One of my favourite *Drive On* contributions is an open letter written by Stacey to her young daughter, Chesnee. Here is an excerpt from Stacey's *"Dear Chesnee"* letter:

"Someday you will hear about how I have a rod and five screws in my back, and that, for seven and a half years when I was a little girl, I had to wear a back brace all day, every day, even when I was sleeping. I could only take it off to play golf. I hated that experience. It was gruelling mentally, physically, emotionally, but it really forged me into who I am today. I'm better when my back is to the wall. I hope my example teaches you to find a way to embrace adversity in your life and turn it into a positive".

....

At the time of writing (October 2021), US golfer Patrick Cantlay is riding high. He scored three-and-a-half points out of four at the recent Ryder Cup. In September he won the Tour Championship and topped the FedEx Cup, pocketing a $15million season *"bonus"*. He is currently ranked fourth in the Official World Golf Rankings. However, Patrick's journey to the upper reaches of world golf has not been easy. In fact, it has been extremely painful, in every way.

In 2011-12 Patrick spent over 50 weeks as the highest ranked male amateur golfer in the world. He was lowest scoring amateur in the 2011 US Open and one week later he shot 60 at the Travelers Championship – the lowest round by an amateur golfer in the 80-year history of the PGA Tour.

Patrick turned professional in 2012. He won the Colombia Championship on the Web.com tour in March 2013, winning a right to play on the full PGA Tour in 2014. Patrick's career was on the up and up.

Two months later it all came crashing down when Patrick injured his back when warming up at a tournament. The pain was extreme and didn't go away. Patrick spent many months searching for a convincing and definite diagnosis. He was eventually diagnosed with a stress fracture in one of his vertebrae. The injury was so bad that Patrick played in only five tournaments in the 2013-14 season. He didn't play any in 2015. Patrick's promising career had stalled.

Patrick stuck diligently to his rehabilitation programme over the weeks, months and years. He planned to return to the tour in early 2016 but severe back pain returned, along with shooting pains in his legs. He was advised not to play for at least ten more months.

Just when Patrick felt things couldn't get much worse, tragedy struck. In February 2016, Patrick was crossing a road in Newport Beach, California with his friend and caddy, Chris Roth, when Chris was hit by a speeding car. Tragically, Chris died in hospital a few hours later. Naturally, Patrick, who was already feeling low about his career, became very depressed.

Patrick returned to the PGA Tour in 2017 and won his first PGA Tour event, the Shriners Open, in November of that year. After winning he said:

"...there were some really low times, and I'd say I'm better for it, as tough as those moments were".

> **SOME GOLFERS ENDURE YEARS OF PAIN AND DISCOMFORT JUST TO MAKE IT TO THE FIRST-TEE. THEIR ENDURANCE, PATIENCE AND COURAGE MAKES THEM FIRST-TEE WINNERS.**

THE SUPERSTAR AND THE SLUMP

In over 160 years of tournament golf there has never been a teenage golfer quite like Lydia Ko. Here is a brief summary of the stellar teenage career of the New Zealand golfing superstar…

January 2012 –won the Women's NSW Open on the ALPG tour aged 14 years-old, becoming the youngest person ever to win a professional golf tour event.

August 2012 –won the CN Canadian Women's Open aged 15-years and four months, becoming the youngest ever winner of an LPGA Tour Event.

Lydia achieved both of the above feats as an amateur!

October 2013 – turned professional.

2014 – won three events.

2015 – won five events.

February 2015 – became the No1 ranked woman golfer in the world and the youngest player ever (by four years!) to top any world golf ranking. She stayed there for 85 consecutive weeks!

September 2015 – won the Evian Championship, aged 18-years and four months, to become the youngest major champion in LPGA Tour history and the youngest major winner for almost 150 years.

March 2016 – won another tournament!

April 2016 – won another major, the ANA Inspiration, to become the youngest double major winner in the history of golf.

June 2016 – won another tournament!

July 2016 – yes, you've guessed it...Lydia won again!

Then, Lydia Ko, the teenage winning machine did something that seemed quite incredible...**SHE STOPPED WINNING...**

2017 – 26 events. 0 wins.

2018 – 26 events. 1 win (in April, at the LPGA Mediheal Championship).

2019 – 24 events. 0 wins.

2020 – 13 events. 0 wins.

Lydia did win again at Lotte Championship in April 2021...more than 1000 days after her previous victory!

What happened to the teenage superstar? Did that early success go to her head? Did she become complacent? Did she stop practising because she was much too busy spending all of her prizemoney? No. No. And no.

The truth is that Lydia worked harder than ever during her *"slump"*. She searched hard to find the perfect caddy partnership. She changed coaches in her relentless pursuit to get even better. She changed equipment. She re-modelled her swing. She worked her socks off.

In a sense, Lydia worked too hard. After so much early success, she felt pressured to keep winning. The expectations she had for herself suddenly began to weigh her down. She started to fear failure. Her confidence slumped. Lydia fell out of the Top 50 in the women's world rankings.

But through her slump, Lydia has learned a lot about golf, herself and life. In 2020, as part of the LPGA's *Drive On* campaign, Lydia wrote an open letter to her 15-year-old self, which included this:

"Reaching world No.1 is exciting and will teach you a lot. But going through change, struggling with your game and wrestling with some tough choices you have to make, that is the fertile ground where growth occurs".

FIRST-TEE WINNERS LEARN MORE (ABOUT GOLF, THEMSELVES AND LIFE) FROM THEIR LOSSES, AND THEIR SLUMPS, THAN THEY DO FROM THEIR VICTORIES.

FROM *"CLEAN UP"* TO THE CLARET JUG

Paul Lawrie has enjoyed an impressive career in golf, winning the 1999 Open Championship, playing with distinction in two Ryder Cup matches and winning a total of eight European Tour titles. Not bad...not bad, at all!

The amazing thing about Paul's story is that, unlike Lydia Ko, he was not a teenage golfing sensation - very far from it. When he was 15 years-old, Paul had a handicap of around eight or nine. When, aged 17 years-old, he got a job as Assistant Professional at Banchory Golf Club (near Aberdeen) Paul's handicap was five, the upper limit to become a professional.

Paul had never won the Scottish Boys Championship – he hadn't even played in it! Paul had never represented Scotland at Boys, Youths or Full International level. His ball-striking was nothing special. He hit every single shot very low and left to right. Paul was a decent club golfer but a million miles from being a major champion or Ryder Cup player and he freely admits this in his autobiography.

When Paul started his Assistant Professional job in April 1986, the Head Professional, Douglas Smart, introduced him to his *"new best friends"* – a vacuum cleaner and a duster. Every morning, Paul had to vacuum every inch of the club shop and polish all the drivers. Paul's pay was £36 per week.

Paul was ambitious to improve his golf game. He immediately embarked on a new regime. Each morning, Paul arrived at the club at 7am and hit balls before opening the shop at 8am. During his hour-long lunch breaks he would have a quick sandwich and hit balls. Whenever his boss, Douglas, would allow it, Paul headed to the range. Straight after closing the shop, he was back on the range or playing matches on the course with fellow pros from local courses. Paul believes he hit at least 600 balls every day during that time. He wore out the grooves of his favourite clubs, his seven and nine irons.

Seven weeks after turning pro, Paul won the first professional event that he entered, winning £300 in the Moray Seafoods Open. He felt like a millionaire!

Paul wanted to get better. He got professional coaching to iron out his too-steep swing and to learn to hit the ball much higher. He honed his skills around the practise green, earning the nickname *"Chippy"* because of his great short game.

Paul progressed and, in 1990, won the Scottish Assistants Championship and Scottish Under-25s Championship. He moved on to competing successfully in Tartan Tour events and, in 1992, he won the Scottish PGA Championship. In that year he qualified to play on the European Tour, where he went on to compete in 620 events over 28 straight years.

Paul's greatest victory came in 1999 when he won The Open Championship, in a play-off against Jean van de Velde and Justin Leonard. Many golf commentators and writers have said that Paul was lucky to win The Open because Jean van de Velde had a two-shot lead with one hole to play of his final round, but proceeded to take seven after a series of reckless decisions and poor shots that saw him paddling in Carnoustie's infamous Barry Burn. It is absolutely true that Paul benefitted from Jean's serious errors. But, every Open champion since 1860 has benefitted from the mistakes of his opponents!

The fact is that a five-handicap Assistant Professional, who spent a lot of his time dusting golf clubs, went on to have his very own Claret Jug to dust! To me, that's a much better story than the one about the player who could have won The Open, but didn't. The lad who couldn't even get a nine-iron shot into the air went on to play in two Ryder Cup matches, winning his singles matches in both. The £36 per week boy became a golfing millionaire. Paul finishes his autobiography with:

"I've been on the European Tour since 1992. I've never lost my card. I've won seven times, including one major championship. I've been in the top-20 of the Order of Merit numerous times. And I've played in two Ryder Cups... I'm proud of all that I've achieved".

> **WHAT FIRST-TEE WINNERS MAY LACK IN *"NATURAL TALENT",* THEY MORE THAN MAKE UP FOR WITH HARD WORK.**

SMELLY SHOES AND SUPER SONS

During my research for this book, I had a great chat with Sam Sloan, an Edinburgh man and a very active member of Blind Golf Scotland. Sam suffers from retinitis pigmentosa (RP), which is a rare genetic disorder of the retina, the specialised light-sensitive tissue at the back of the eye. When he is addressing the ball, Sam can see only a blurred image of the ball and his clubhead. The heads of his clubs are painted white to help him see them as clearly as possible. Sam cannot see his ball in flight and can only see a very unclear image of the hole ahead, so he needs a guide to help him play golf.

Sam was already Visually Impaired (VI) when he took up golf at the request of his ten-year-old son who wanted his Dad to play with him. Sam's first score was 135 but he was determined to get better and he started to get lessons. He has got much, much better over the years.

Sam has had a lot of fun playing in the VI world championship in many exciting locations. Whilst competing in Japan, Sam and a large group of fellow competitors went for a meal in a restaurant, where customers had to take their shoes off before eating. The shoes were all placed on a rack. After a beer, Sam got up to go to the toilet, didn't see the shoe rack and knocked it over, spreading about twenty-five pairs of shoes across the floor. The next twenty minutes was spent with Sam and his fellow VI golfers sniffing shoes to try to identify which were theirs. I immediately felt guilty when I laughed at that story but Sam said it was ok, as it was funny! Golf has provided Sam with lots of laughs.

Sam was very keen to stress to me that VI golfers are no different from any other golfers:

"There is nothing special about visually impaired golfers. We still go for lessons. We are still competitive. We want to win. We don't just turn up and play. The competition is fierce. Sometimes we even fall-out, but a few minutes later it's forgotten. We always finish with a drink and a good laugh in the clubhouse".

Despite his exotic golfing trips, Sam said his favourite thing in golf is playing with his sons, just along the road in Edinburgh:

"There is nothing better in golf than playing with my two boys, Scott and Fraser. I love the crack playing golf with my sons and their pals".

> **IF YOU ARRIVE AT THE FIRST-TEE WITH THE SAME SENSE OF ENTHUSIASM, GRATITUDE, FRIENDLINESS AND FUN AS SAM YOU WON'T ALWAYS HAVE A GOOD ROUND, BUT YOU WILL ALWAYS HAVE A GOOD DAY.**

GERRY'S VISION

Visually Impaired (VI) golf in the UK owes a great deal to the determination and vision of Gerry Kelly, who I had the pleasure of chatting with whilst doing research for this book.

Gerry was diagnosed with Stargardt Disease, a progressive disease of the retina, in 1971. Gerry was registered blind in 1980 and, in that year, he was medically retired from his managerial job with ICI Petrochemicals. He never expected to be retired at 40 years of age.

Gerry started looking for a new job as well as a completely new challenge. Gerry remembered reading an article about a blind American golfer called Pat Browne Jnr who had visited Scotland to play the country's most famous courses. During his visit, Pat had expressed disappointment that there were no VI Golf Associations in the UK. This felt like a challenge to Gerry and, despite never having golfed before, he decided to try to make contact with other VI people interested in playing, with the view to setting up a golf society.

In an era before social media and the internet, Gerry had to rely on his typewriter and the help of his wife, Mary. He wrote to lots of social work departments, disability organisations and local and national media outlets trying to make contact with VI golfers. Nothing happened.

Later, the Glasgow and West of Scotland Society for the Blind ran an article on Gerry's golfing vision in their audio magazine (*Playback)*. Nothing happened.

Gerry was taken-aback at the negativity that his vision for a VI golf society seemed to provoke; even sports associations for VI people seemed to believe that Gerry's golfing vision was a non-starter.

In 1982, at a computer training event, Gerry shared his golf vision with a VI man called Ron Tomlinson, who immediately came onboard. Gerry requested that the *Playback* magazine re-run his article and this time something did happen – two VI men got in touch saying that they too wanted to try golf.

Around six months later, Auchenharvie Golf Club in Ayrshire offered Gerry and his new golfing buddies associate membership, professional lessons and volunteer guides to assist them. Gerry has said:

"We were so lucky to have met these wonderful people, who believed in us and gave up their Saturday afternoons to assist us".

By the end of 1982 the West of Scotland Visually Impaired Golf Society was officially born...one of the proudest days in Gerry's life. Since then, VI golf in the UK has, slowly but surely, gone from strength to strength. In 1984 the first VI golf international between Scotland and England was played (at Auchenharvie GC). In 1986 the Scottish Blind Golf Society (now Blind Golf Scotland) was established. In 1987 the first ever British Open for Blind Golfers was held in Glasgow, with permission and support from the Royal and Ancient Golf Club.

Gerry has enjoyed playing in events all over the UK and the world but his greatest golfing success came at his desk, on his type-writer, working on turning his vision for VI golf into a reality:

"It was a lifesaver for me, something to get my teeth into. Building it up was fantastic for me and kept me sane. I love organising things, as much as I love playing golf, so it was very, very rewarding".

FOR SOME GOLFERS THE BIGGEST POSSIBLE "*WIN*" IN GOLF IS HELPING OTHERS TO ACCESS THE GAME...AND TO FALL IN LOVE WITH IT.

FIRST-TEE WINNERS SEE POTENTIAL WHERE OTHERS SEE PROBLEMS. THEY SEE EXCITING POSSIBILITIES WHERE OTHERS SEE IMPOSSIBILITIES. THEY SEE ABILITY WHERE OTHERS SEE DISABILITY.

ALISON'S AMERICAN ADVENTURES

The US Women's Open Championship is the oldest, most respected championship in women's golf. When Alison Nicholas won the event in 1997, her ten under par total was a new scoring record for the championship. It sounds like golfing in the USA came easy to English Alison. The truth is that Alison's victory was the culmination of a nine-year stateside struggle.

Alison's first event in the USA came in 1988, a year after she won the Ladies British Open. Alison played in the US Women's Open in Baltimore and finished 64th. She was amazed by...

- the length of the course; it was much longer than she was used to.
- the *"unbelievably difficult"* greens.
- the thickness of the rough, which was hard to hit out of.
- the long driving of the American players, compared to hers.
- the scale of the event; she wasn't used to such *"immense"* crowds.

Alison played a number of tournaments in the USA in 1990. She found it very difficult to adapt to the fast greens and struggled to make delicate chips from the thick, greenside rough. Alison was used to finishing in the Top 10 in European events. On the LPGA tour she struggled to make cuts and make any money. Alison found playing on the long American courses, often in sweltering heat, very tiring. She would often leave the course so tired that she wasn't able to practise afterwards, as she normally would on the European Tour.

The more Alison missed cuts, the more she missed home. She lost confidence, felt miserable and became negative. After yet another missed cut, Alison returned home, thinking that her time on the LPGA tour was over for good.

Alison didn't play many more events in the USA until 1993. This time, she vowed to be more patient. Her performances improved. At the Corning Classic, she was beaten in a sudden death play-off, but her confidence was boosted.

The big turning point for Alison came at the start of 1995 when she decided to get fitter and to re-model her swing. She employed a fitness trainer and failed every one of the initial fitness tests he gave her! Alison committed to a programme of exercises to improve her strength, flexibility and power. She embarked on a healthy eating and weight-loss programme. She also learned breathing exercises to help her manage her on-course nerves.

Alison set to work on re-modelling her swing with her golf coach. She focused on making her backswing less steep and on turning (not dipping) her left shoulder. Her goal was to become more consistent and to hit longer drives, which would help on long American courses. Alison also worked on a variety of chip shots to cope with thick greenside rough.

Week after week Alison worked in the gym and on the driving range, doing *"endless repetitions"* of her new swing as well as her exercises. It was difficult, but she stuck to the task.

Alison's scores did not improve immediately. When she returned to the USA in May 1995, she missed the cut in her first four events! However, she was convinced that she was on the right path to achieving her goal of winning a major. She stuck to the changes she was making to her body and swing. Alison's *"stickability"* was rewarded with two LPGA Tour victories in 1995.

The really big reward came two years later at the US Women's Open – the major victory that Alison had worked towards for so long. In her autobiography, she wrote:

"I have been very fortunate to enjoy the life I have had, but I also put a lot of work into it. Golf is a difficult game and I have struggled at times. You don't play well all of the time, but it is all about persevering".

> **IT IS IMPOSSIBLE TO ACHIEVE A 100% WIN-RATE BUT FIRST-TEE WINNERS ARE 100% COMMITTED TO BECOMING AS GOOD AS THEY CAN BE.**

FROM TANTRUMS TO TROPHIES

When it comes to the four major tournaments, Brooks Koepka has been the best male golfer of the past six years. Since 2015 Brooks has finished in the Top 10 in fifteen majors. Brooks won the 2017 and 2018 US Open Championships and the 2018 and 2019 USPGA titles.

Brooks generally plays much better in the four biggest, most prestigious, events (the majors) than he does in *"ordinary"* tour events. That is very unusual, indeed. The bigger the event, the calmer and more confident Brooks seems to become. Golf commentators have described Brooks as a *"robot"*, an *"ice-man"* and an *"unfeeling killer"* (which seems a wee bit harsh, don't you think?).

Brooks Koepka hasn't always been so ice-cool on the golf course: he used to have golfing tantrums...big, bad tantrums and lots of them!

Brooks used to play for Florida State University golf team. His attitude on the golf course was so negative that the team's assistant coach, Chris Malloy, used to hide amongst the trees to secretly film his temper tantrums. The coach would play the videos to Brooks to show how his swearing, club slamming and self-criticism was negatively affecting his game. It made no difference.

Brooks' attitude on the course started to improve when Coach Malloy started punishing all of the golf team for Brooks' bad behaviour by making everyone run the steps of the university football stadium. Brooks didn't want to negatively affect his teammates.

Brooks' behaviour improved even more after a major university championship final in which he got so angry with a bad end to his round that he signed for an incorrect score and was disqualified. He nearly cost his team the championship. This was a wake-up call for Brooks and he began to work much harder on controlling his behaviour on the course.

Here's what Coach Malloy told ESPN in 2019, about Brooks:

"He was the toughest player I ever had to change. He had arguably the worst temper, and was so hard on himself. He was the furthest person from what you see today. He definitely would not have won any majors if he had the same temperament today that he had then".

FIRST-TEE WINNERS LEARN THAT DISPLAYS OF ANGER MAKE THEM PLAY WORSE AND PUT OFF THEIR OPPONENTS, WHICH ISN'T FAIR. THEY LEARN TO CONTROL THEIR ANGER, AS BEST THEY CAN.

"PLAY HAPPY"

Around 1979 (when I was ten years-old) my Mum took me to see a challenge match at Turnberry golf course in Ayrshire featuring four great golfers: Nick Faldo and Mickey Walker versus Lee Trevino and Nancy Lopez. Nancy seemed smiley and friendly and warm. I think I was in love with her (and Chris Evert, the tennis player) for a while!

Nancy won an incredible nine LPGA Tour events in 1978 – her first year on the tour! In all, Nancy won 48 LPGA events during her incredible career, including three majors.

Nancy was an outstanding, determined and extremely focussed golfer who became famous for her calm, fun-loving, smiley attitude on the course. Nancy has said:

"My Dad taught me never to give up and to play the game with love and respect and to just go out there and have fun. My Dad always said 'play happy' and that was my goal all of the time and that helped me get through a bad round when I wasn't playing well...When you get angry internally and you're mad and you look mad and frustrated it shows in your golf game and my Dad always taught me not to do that".

In her book, *The Education of a Woman Golfer,* Nancy wrote this:

"If a wasted shot or a poor round keeps gnawing away at your mind and spirit, it's going to affect your next shot or your next round. If you don't let it, it won't...All the gnashing of teeth in the world isn't going to change that double-bogey -6 into the par 4 you should have made...About all I do after a bad hole is draw a little fence around the figure on my scorecard, so it won't spill over onto the next hole!".

If you search *"Nancy Lopez images"* on the internet you will see a lot of smiles...and Nancy isn't holding a trophy in all of them!

FIRST-TEE WINNERS ARRIVE AT THE FIRST-TEE DETERMINED TO WIN. THEY ARE EQUALLY DETERMINED TO TRY TO HAVE FUN, STAY AS CALM AS POSSIBLE AND FEEL GOOD ABOUT THEMSELVES ...WIN, LOSE OR DRAW.

THE ONE-CLUB WONDER

The late Seve Ballesteros is widely regarded as having been the most creative and imaginative golfer of all time, especially around the greens. Seve played thousands of wonderful, almost miraculous, shots in his lifetime. He had an almost unique ability to *"see"*, and pull-off, wonderful shots that many other top professionals couldn't even imagine.

Seve was born into a very poor, farming family in a village called Padrena in northern Spain. His family's small farm overlooked a golf course and Seve was fascinated by the game from a young age; his older brothers all caddied at the club and his uncle was a professional. Seve was too young to join the club and, in any case, his family could not afford the membership fees.

By age eight, Seve owned his first golf club – a three-iron. Seve practised with this club (and balls he found on the golf course) for hours on the local beach. He set up a little mini course in one of his parents' fields with tomato tins for holes. In the evening, when it was close to darkness and the course was empty, Seve and his brothers would sneak on and play the par three hole that sat close to their garden. When it got much too dark, Seve would move on to the barn where he hit shots into fishing nets that he had hung from the ceiling.

Given that he had only a three-iron, which is a long club with very little loft, Seve had to develop creative ways to play lots of different shots, especially his pitches, chips and putts. Seve's uniquely wonderful imagination, and ability to *"see"* and play shots that others couldn't even dream of, was developed on the beach, in a field and in the half-darkness...all with one club!

Seve went on to become a great champion and global golfing superstar. Even then, Seve often practised his short game with his longer, less-lofted clubs. Tiger Woods tells a story about watching Seve practising brilliant bunker shots with a three-iron many, many years after he <u>had</u> to! Seve didn't want to lose the wonderful skills of creativity and imagination that he had developed as a boy.

> **FIRST-TEE WINNERS DON'T SIT AROUND WAITING FOR PERFECT EQUIPMENT OR IDEAL CIRCUMSTANCES. THEY MAKE THE MOST OF WHAT THEY HAVE GOT.**

> **FIRST-TEE WINNERS JUST LOVE TO PLAY GOLF - IT EXCITES THEIR IMAGINATION!**

DEFINETELY NOT A BLAND VICTORY

One of my favourite golfing stories of recent years features an English professional golfer called Richard Bland. Despite his name, I don't think there is anything bland or boring about his story - it's inspirational, especially to an oldie like me!

Richard has been a "journeyman" tournament professional since 1996; he has played steadily and made a decent living, without doing anything outstanding. All of that changed in May 2021 at the British Masters at The Belfry, England. Richard shot thirteen under par for four rounds (including a final round 66), tied first with Italy's Guido Migliozzi and beat him in a sudden-death play-off.

Richard had finally won his first European Tour event, 23 years after he played in his first one...and at his 478th attempt! That's right, Richard had previously played 477 European Tour events without a win!

At 48 years-old, Richard became the oldest first-time winner in the almost 50-year history of the European Tour. He won the biggest cheque of his golfing career – almost 340,000 Euros. His win earned him a spot in the US Open in June 2021, where he led after two rounds, becoming the oldest two-round leader in US Open history.

What makes Richard's achievement all the more remarkable, and inspiring, is that on four separate occasions he has lost his playing rights for the European Tour and has re-earned them on the lower, less lucrative Challenge Tour. This happened most recently when Richard lost his European Tour card in 2018. He went back to the lower Challenge Tour and re-graduated from it in 2019, when he was aged 46 years old. Many (probably most!) golfers of that age would have given in but here's what Richard said after his British Masters victory:

"I don't quit. Even if I'm having a bad day – you might be frustrated by it – but you never throw in the towel because you never know in this game what's round the corner".

There was another element to Richard's British Masters victory that made it extra-special. Seconds after winning the play-off, Richard was interviewed by Sky Sports presenter Tim Barter, who has also been Richard's close friend and golf coach for the past twenty years. The two men embraced and both were close to tears. Here's what Richard said about Tim:

"To have him here on the 18th green with me makes it extra special. This is much his as it is mine, with the work we've put in. He's always believed in me more than I believed in myself, he's always been telling me that. It's paid off".

I think it was pretty classy of Richard to give so much credit to his friend and golf coach at the very moment of his first ever victory.

With one win in almost 500 European Tour events, Richard Bland has a win-rate of around 0.2%. That doesn't sound too impressive as a statistic. However, some of the most important things in golf, sport and life cannot be translated into a percentage or a digit or a statistic; things like patience, perseverance, gratitude and grit. If they could, Richard Bland's *"stats"* would be very impressive indeed.

> **FIRST-TEE WINNERS KEEP COMING BACK TO THE FIRST-TEE, TIME AND TIME AND TIME AGAIN. EACH TIME THEY BRING WITH THEM RENEWED OPTIMISM, ENTHUSIASM AND DETERMINATION.**

> **FIRST-TEE WINNERS ARE GRATEFUL FOR ALL THE HELP THAT THEY GET - AND THEY SHOW IT!**

DAVE

When I was a junior golfer, the Junior Convenor of my home club was called Dave. Dave was a high school teacher and was also in charge of all the school's golf activities. Between the golf club and school golf, Dave dedicated a lot of his time and energy to the development of junior golf. He organised all of the golf club's junior events, sourced prizes, tracked handicaps and goodness knows what else he did behind the scenes. He took us to numerous exotic locations, such as Ayrshire and Kirkcudbrightshire, to play in school golf events; to be fair, this was probably a welcome break for him from teaching woodwork!

Dave was dedicated to helping juniors to improve their skills and enjoy the game as much as possible. There were no golf professionals in our remote corner of Scotland. There was an open prison near our town and Dave somehow learned that one of the prisoners was a scratch golfer. Dave negotiated with the prison governor and gained permission for the prisoner (whose crime, I think, had been financial not physical) to give golf lessons to juniors in the school hall, smashing real golf balls into nets. The prisoner clearly got a sense of satisfaction from teaching us and it helped us greatly.

Dave was a golf nut. He seemed to have thousands of golf stories and loved to tell them all. His passion for the game was obvious and infectious. Dave was a decent golfer – around ten in handicap. He could have been much better than that but it is difficult to achieve your golfing potential when you spend so much of your time and energy on providing opportunities for other players.

Sadly, Dave passed away quite a few years ago at quite a young age. It is almost forty years since he took us to those school golf events, set up those lessons from the prisoner and spent hours organising junior medals. I still remember him very fondly and I'm still grateful for all that he did for me. I can see no reason why I won't feel that way for the rest of my life.

I wonder if golf's Junior Convenors know what a profoundly positive, and permanent, impact they have on the lives of other players? In encouraging, educating and enthusing young players, they create a golfing legacy as great as any champion golfer ever has.

> **SOME GOLFERS NEVER REACH THEIR FULL PLAYING POTENTIAL BECAUSE THEY ARE SO BUSY HELPING OTHERS TO REACH THEIRS. THEY ARE "*WINNERS*". I HOPE THEY KNOW HOW IMPORTANT THEY ARE.**

GOLF'S MOST HUMBLE CHAMPION

If any golfer has good reason to be a big-headed, boastful bragger it's Kathy Whitworth. Thanks to the 88 professional tour victories she secured between 1962 and 1985, Kathy is golf's *"winningest"* ever professional player; no-one, male or female, has won as many tournaments as she.

Here are some more of Kathy's incredible achievements:

- Eight times winner of the LPGA Tour money list.
- Seven times LPGA *"Player of the Year"*.
- Winner of six major championships.
- First woman to win over $1 million in career prizemoney (doing so in 1981)

I think you'll agree that this is a pretty decent record for someone who took up the game at 15 years-old (using her late grandfather's clubs) and who was so poor in her first season that she was embarrassed to play with other golfers.

Kathy's record is all the more impressive for the fact that in her rookie (first) year on the tour she had a terrible scoring average of 80. In 26 tournaments she earned a measly $1217. She went home to Jal, New Mexico to tell her Mum and Dad that she wasn't good enough for the tour and was going to give up. They promptly told her to keep trying for at least three more years. Mr and Mrs Whitworth were clearly very wise, indeed...or they owned a crystal ball!

Truthfully, I had never heard of Kathy Whitworth until recently. I'm glad I've discovered her as I love her story. What

I love most of all about Kathy's story is that golf's most *"winningest"* player is not a big-headed, boastful bragger at all. In fact, Kathy is widely considered to be one of the most humble champions in sport. For example, here is what Kathy once told Lisa D. Mickey in a *Golf World* interview:

"A lot of times, I didn't win; somebody else just lost".

On her 88 tour victories she said this:

"This is a record the LPGA has. I'm more proud of that for them than I am for myself".

Kathy was inducted into the World Golf Hall of Fame in 1982. This quote from her appears on her biography on their site:

"I'm not some great oddity. I was just fortunate to be so successful. What I did in being a better player does not make me a better person. When I'm asked how I would like to be remembered, I feel that if people remember me at all, it will be good enough".

Renee Powell was, after Althea Gibson, the second African-American woman to compete on the LPGA Tour, joining it in 1967. She experienced much discrimination along the way. Renee recalls arriving at a hotel in Idaho prior to an event, along with other players, including Kathy Whitworth. Of the 30 or 40 reservations made by the players, only one was mysteriously missing – that of Renee, who was told by hotel staff to look elsewhere. Renee recalls that it was Kathy who went to the reception desk and stated: *"Either she stays...or we all go!"*. Renee's reservation instantly appeared!

Fellow top pro, Betsy Rawls said this about Kathy:

"She was wonderful to play with- sweet as could be, nice to everybody..."

Kathy was coached by a famous Texan golf teacher called Harvey Penick, who said this about her:

"Kathy Whitworth is one of the sweetest and most thoughtful people I ever knew...There's no nicer person on earth than Kathy".

> **FIRST-TEE WINNERS DO NOT FEEL A NEED TO BOAST OR BRAG OR BRING-DOWN THEIR FELLOW COMPETITORS. THEY ARE KIND TO OTHER PLAYERS...WHILST TRYING VERY HARD TO BEAT THEM!**

RORY'S RYDER CUP REGRETS

As I write this, the dust is settling on the most recent Ryder Cup match, a thumping 19-9 home victory for the USA against Europe. Many of the European team players performed well below their best from the outset. By the end of day one (of three) it seemed almost inevitable that the USA would coast to victory on the Whistling Straits course...and they did.

Northern Ireland's Rory McIlroy, the only multiple-major winner on the European team, played extremely poorly for the first two days. Rory lost two doubles matches (with Ian Poulter and Shane Lowry) on day one; he had never before lost twice in a day at a Ryder Cup.

On the morning of day two, Rory was dropped from the foursomes matches – the first time he had ever been left out of a set of Ryder Cup matches. That afternoon, Rory lost again (playing with Ian Poulter). In all three of these matches, Rory and his respective partners were beaten soundly, failing to get beyond the fifteenth green each time.

Rory reclaimed some professional pride on the final day of the event when he won the opening match of the singles against Xander Schauffele. However, from the other match scores at that point, it was clear that Europe was heading towards a very heavy defeat.

What happened two minutes after Rory's match finished was, for me, the highlight of the whole event. Rory was interviewed by Henni Koyack of Sky Sports and, fighting tears, he said this:

"I love being part of this team. I love my team-mates so much. I should have done more for them this week. I'm glad I put a point on the board for Europe today but I just can't wait to get another shot at this. It is, by far, the best experience in golf...and I hope little boys and girls watching this today aspire to play in this event, or the Solheim Cup, because there's nothing better than being part of a team...I'm proud of every single one of these players that played this week. I'm proud of our Captain and-Vice Captains...it's been a tough week".

I think it is incredible that a top-class professional golfer, and multi-millionaire, like Rory, could care so much about an event in which there is no prizemoney to be won.

I think it is wonderful that a golfer who has won almost 30 international events on his own, and has spent over 100 weeks as the world's No1 male player, could feel so terribly disappointed at letting his team mates down, and that his own singles victory couldn't ease that pain in any way.

I think it is fascinating, and strangely heart-warming, that a man who has experienced so much individual glory (in what is a very individual sport) believes that the Ryder Cup, a team event, is *"the best experience in golf"*.

I love that Rory talked about loving his team mates. That is the kind of raw, personal and honest language we don't often hear from sporting superstars, especially male ones.

I love that Rory recognised, and felt proud of, the effort of his team mates, captain and vice-captains, even in defeat.

Above all, I love that, in a moment of high emotion and great disappointment, Rory's instinct was to think of junior golfers and to say something that would inspire them to strive for glory; team glory, specifically. It was also great that he mentioned the Solheim Cup - the biennial match between the best women professionals from the USA and Europe - clearly showing he believes that too is a hugely important event.

Rory's golf at Whistling Straits was very poor by his incredible standards. His three losses in four games certainly contributed significantly to Europe's downfall. Rory's golf let him down but his words certainly did not. His interview was the most powerful and touching TV golf interview I've seen in 40 years as a viewer. He spoke with humility, pride, passion, gratitude, regret, honesty and love. He lost three games out of four and was part of a losing team, but in one very short, tearful, heartfelt interview Rory McIlroy proved that...

YOU CAN WIN AT GOLF...EVEN WHEN YOU LOSE.

F.I.R.S.T-T.E.E WINNER

FRIENDLY (and Fun!)

INDEPENDENT (a golfer who thinks for him/herself)

RESPECTFUL (of the course, the rules and other players)

SERIOUS (about improving)

TENACIOUS

THANKS PEOPLE (for their help)

EVEN-TEMPERED (not easily made angry)

ENTHUSIASTIC

GOLFING MEMORIES AND GOLFING FRIENDS

From the age of around 10 years-old to my mid-20s, I was a member of a small golf club in Galloway. I got down to a decent handicap, won a trophy or two along the way and shot some good scores. I can't really remember any details beyond that!

Strangely, I can very vividly remember playing pool in the clubhouse with one of the adult members when I was around 13 years-old. I was calling him *"Mr Campbell"*, partly because that was his name(!) and partly because my Mum and Dad had brought me up to be very polite to adults. I can distinctly remember *"Mr Campbell"* asking me to call him *"Jim"* and, from that day on, I did.

I freely admit that my Mr Campbell/Jim story isn't a classic! However, forty years later, I can still clearly remember it happening! I wonder why? To answer my own question, I think it was because it meant a lot to 13 years-old me that a prominent adult member (Jim had been captain and was a permanent fixture on the club's committee and in the "A" team) wanted me to address him as a friend would. That was a big thing to me!

I can also remember that Jim used his influence in the committee to ensure that the low handicap junior members got to compete for the "A" team in the inter-club summer league; he clearly agreed with the philosophy of the football manager, Sir Matt Busby, that *"If you are good enough, you are old enough"*.

Jim strongly advocated that the juniors who represented the club in league matches should have their after-match meals paid for by the club. Some of his fellow committee members weren't too keen on that idea, from what I heard, but Jim won the argument. Over the years, dozens of juniors benefitted from Jim's forward-thinking and inclusive attitude.

I'm a golf nut and have been very serious about my golf through the years. It intrigues me that I can't recall a single round from my fifteen golfing years in Galloway but I can recall my wee game of pool with Jim and all that he did to allow me and other juniors to have a chance to play for the club. Most of all, I can remember what a decent, likeable and fun man Jim was. Sadly, he is no longer with us, but I won't ever forget him.

Based on how my brain works, I can only assume that our most vivid and meaningful golfing memories are not of shots or scores or even our successes but are of the golfers we meet during our golfing journey. The kinder, friendlier and more supportive those people are, the more deeply-embedded, and precious, our memories of them seem to be.

In a similar vein, I played a number of great golf courses with my Dad, including the iconic Old Course at St. Andrews, the majestic Kings Course at Gleneagles and the visually stunning Kingsbarns (described by my Dad as *"golfing heaven"* as he walked off the 18th green). However, my clearest and dearest memory of our golfing adventures is of us sitting having a fish supper in a public garden in Tain during a Highland golfing trip! No scorecard or out-of-bounds or left-to-right downhill three-footers to worry about, just two golfing pals – and a father and son – enjoying time together on a beautiful summer's evening.

As I write this, it is mid-October 2021 and another golf season is grinding to a halt. I shot my personal best on the course this year, got my handicap down by one shot and won a voucher at an open (that hasn't happened in years!).

However, I think the memory from this season that will linger longest was a day out on the gorgeous links of Northumberland with two golfing pals, Nathan and Colin. Fine weather, two beautifully scenic courses and great banter – finished off with a fish supper (again!) on the way home. Hard to beat!

I want to win golf competitions. When I'm in my 90s and shuffling around the green on my walking frame, I'll still want to win golf competitions. However, as I get older, I'm starting to think that there's much more to *"winning at golf"* than trophies. I must be getting majorly soppy, because I genuinely believe that...

ANY GOLFER WHO ARRIVES AT THE FIRST-TEE WITH A FRIEND, OR WALKS OFF THE FINAL GREEN WITH A NEW FRIEND, IS A *"WINNER".*

SOURCES

23 Out of 100 is Awesome: John Hawkins, Why Annika Sorenstam is the Most Dominant Golfer Ever – Male or Female, si.com, 4/08/21 AND Nelly Korda bio, lpga.com AND Gareth Hanna, Is Rory McIlroy really a bad "closer"?, belfasttelegraph.co.uk, 9/3/20.

The 10,000% Golfer: Dylan Dethier, Tiger Woods' 10 was a disaster, but his response was more important, golf.com, 15/11/20 AND Tiger Woods (with Lorne Rubenstein), Unprecedented: The Masters and Me, Sphere, 2007.

The Little Girl Who Missed her Putts...on Purpose!: Association for Applied Sports Psychology, AASP 2017 Keynote: An Interview with Performance Excellence Award Winner Annika Sorenstam, 22/1/19 on YouTube.

The Jug and the Jacket:The Open, Adam Scott reveals his disappointment after his final round at the 2012 Open, on YouTube, 23/07/12 AND Martin Samuel, Scott's Open loss was a brutal capitulation played out in frozen moments of horror, dailymail.co.uk, 22/07/12

From Masters Crash to Masterclass: The Telegraph.co.uk, Rory McIlroy on his disastrous Masters 2011 meltdown, 13/4/21 on YouTube.(including quote) AND Frank Worrall, Rory McIlroy: The Champion Golfer, John Blake Publishing Ltd, 2014.

No Hammer Required: European Tour, Justin Rose, Life on Tour Podcast, Episode 4, on YouTube, 25/07/18 AND John Boon, Smelling of Roses, thesun.co.uk, 9/4,21.

Beating the Bullies: Haley Moore bio, arizonawildcats.com AND Tim Reynolds, From bullied to birdies: Haley Moore's LPGA story resonates, abcnews.go.com, 26/11/20 AND NCAA Golf, Haley Moore's inspiring Story, Golf Channel video on facebook.com, 19/05/19 AND Good Morning America, Rookie pro golfer Haley Moore on how she made it to the LGPA (sic), on YouTube, 15/12/20 AND Haley Moore, The Strength you Build (part of the Drive On campaign), lpga.com, 4/08/20.

Heads Held High: Darren Clarke, An Open Book: My Autobiography, Hodder and Stoughton, 2012 AND Press Association, Brian Davis has no regrets calling two-shot penalty on himself, guardian.com, 19/4/10 AND integrity *darren Clarke,* posted on YouTube by aleikem , 27/05/2006 (includes footage from Sky Sports).

"Nice Guys Finish Last…Blah, Blah, Blah": Greg Norman, *The Way of the Shark*, Ebury Press, 2006 AND Laura Davies (with Lewine Mair), *Laura Davies; Naturally…*, Bloomsbury Publishing Plc, 1996 AND Lee Trevino (with Sam Blair), *Super Mex: An Autobiography*, Stanley Paul and Co. Ltd, 1983 AND Gary Player, *The Golfer's Guide to the Meaning of Life*, Rodale Inc, 2001. AND John Feinstein, *With Age, Jack Nicklaus' legacy becomes less defined by his record and more by his character*, golfdigest.com, 20/1/20 (including the Tom Watson quote) AND Jak Nicklaus bio, Wikipedia.com.

"The Concession": Nick Callow, *The History of the Ryder Cup (The Definitive Record of Golf's Greatest Tournament)*, Sevenoaks/Carlton Books Ltd.2014 (Including the Jack Nicklaus quote) AND Peter Burns (with Ed Hodge), *Behind the Ryder Cup (The Players' Stories)*, Polaris Publishing Ltd, 2016. (Including the Sam Snead quote).

Tiger's "Grandpa Charlie": Pete McDaniel, *Uneven Lies: The Heroic Story of African-Americans in Golf*, The American Golfer Inc., 2000 (both Charlie Sifford quotes and the Tiger Woods quote from this book) AND Nancy Churnin, *Charlie Takes His Shot*, Albert Whitman and Company, 2018 AND Lyle Slovick, *Trials and Triumphs of Golf's Greatest Champion (A Legacy of Hope)*, Rowman and Littlefield Publishers, Inc., 2016 AND Tiger Woods (with Lorne Rubenstein), *Unprecedented: The Masters and Me*, Sphere, 2007 AND Farrell Evans, *Sifford's legacy honored by a nation*, espn.co.uk, 11/11/14.

Painful Journeys: Stacey Lewis, *Dear Chesnee* (open letter, part of the *Drive On* Campaign), lpga.com, 23/06/21 AND Luke Norris, *How Patrick Cantlay Overcame Injury and Tragedy to Become one of the Best Golfers in the World*, sportscasting.com, 21/04/20 AND Mike Stachura, *Patrick Cantlay: A Comeback from Nowhere*, golfdigest.com, 13/04/19 AND Kevin Casey, *What Patrick Cantlay said after winning the Shriners Open*, golfweek.usatoday.com, 5/11/17.

The Superstar and the Slump: Alex Myers, *9 Lydia Ko stats that will make your jaw drop*, golfdigest.com, 27/04/15 AND Lydia Ko, *Letter to My 15-year-old Self* (open letter, part of the *Drive On* campaign), lpga.com,

16/07/20 AND Dylan Dethier, *Lydia Ko wrote herself a 3-word note – we'd do well to follow her advice*, golf.com, 18/04/21 AND Jessica Marksbury, *How a shift in mindset helped Lydia Ko end her winless drought*, gof.com, 10/6/21 AND Des Beiler, *Ex-coach blames Lydia Ko's slumping career on her parents*, thespec.com, 03/03/20.

From *"Clean Up"* to Claret Jug: Paul Lawrie (with John Huggan), *An Open Book: The Paul Lawrie Story*, The Derby Books Publishing Company Ltd, 2012.

Gerry's Vision: Gerry T. Kelly, *A brief insight of my journey to establish golf for the blind*, scottishblindgolf.com.

Alison's American Adventures: Alison Nicholas (with Madeleine Winnett), *Walking Tall*, Bennion Kearney Ltd, 2015.

From Tantrums to Trophies: Ian O'Connor, *Even when there was doubt, Brooks Koepka had no doubt*, espn.co.uk, 19/05/19.

Play Happy": NCPGA, *Nancy Lopez Interview*, 22/10/14 on YouTube (including first quote) AND Nancy Lopez (with Peter Schwed), *The Education of a Woman Golfer*, Simon and Schuster, 1979.

The One Club Wonder: Seve Ballesteros, *Seve; The Official Autobiography*, Yellow Jersey Press, 2008 AND *Tiger Woods recalls Seve Ballesteros bunker masterclass*, bbc.co.uk/sport, 5/07/2011.

Definitely Not a Bland Victory: No named author, *Bland proves that dreams do come true*, europeantour.com, 15/05/21.

Golf's Most Humble Champion: Sheri Wilson, *Kathy Whitworth- a golf legend turns 80, pushes ahead*, primewomen.com, 14/09/year not stated AND Barry McDermott, *Wrong Image but the Right Touch*, vault.si.com (Sports Illustrated archive), 25/7/83 AND Lisa D. Mickey, *Tiger's feat is remarkable, but don't forget golf's winningest player, Kathy Whitworth*, espn.co.uk, 29/10/19 (the first two highlighted Kathy Whitworth quotes, from Golf World magazine, are referenced in this article) AND Ron Sirak, *A Legend like No Other*, golfdigest.com, 29/06/09 (including Betsy Rawls quote) AND *Kathy Whitworth Bio*, worldgolfhalloffame.org, not dated, (including Kathy Whitworth quote *"I'm no oddity..."*) AND Randall Mell,

Struggle for Equality binds Kathy Whitworth, Renee Powell, golfchannel.com, 18/03/14 AND Beth Ann Nichols, *A toast to Kathy Whitworth, the world's easiest interview,* golfweek.usatoday.com, 6/10/19 AND Harvey Penick (with Bud Shrake), *Harvey Penick's Little Red Golf Book (Lessons and Teachings from a Lifetime in Golf),* Collins Willow, 1993 AND David Spada, *Kathy Whitworth,* video on YouTube (based on Sports and Torts Radio Show interview with Kathy Whitworth by David Spada and Elliott Harris), 29/06/12.